A Fake Stone

Copyright © 2017 Lokendra Porush Kumar

First Edition October 2017

ISBN-13: 978-1527214002 (FNV Publications)

ISBN-10: 1527214001

A catalogue record for this book is available from the British Library.

Cover Design by © Chiara Designs (girardelli.chiara@gmail.com)

All Inside illustrations by © Betibup33 (betibup33@gmail.com),

Except illustration ''Diwali Lights'' created by Charu Porush

FNV Publications
London, EC2A 4NE
U.K

Contents

In loving memory of my Mother and my Grandmother

Who both believed in me.

About the author

Lokendra Kumar Porush was born and brought up in a lower middle class family of farmers, in Khonda Hazari, a small village in the district of Hathras, Uttar Pradesh, Northern India.

His early education started in Mahatma Ghandi Inter College, Hathras. He then graduated from PC Bagla Degree College Hathras and subsequently did a Masters in English from the same college affiliated to Bhim Rao Ambedkar University Agra (Agra University).

When he is not teaching, Lokendra, a humorous man by nature is also an ardent thinker and likes writing deep poetry. He also enjoys the odd volleyball match with his students at Jawahar Navodaya Vidyalaya, Agsauli, Uttar Pradesh where he is currently teaching English.

This book is dedicated to his family, especially his mother and grandmother, two women who were a great inspiration to him. With six children to feed, money was scarce in the family, but his mother, recognising early on that her middle child has an aptitude for studies made sure he would get a higher education. She saved whatever money she could scrape together from the household meagre budget and borrowed the rest to send him to university. He always vowed to make her proud of her sacrifices.

His first poetry book, On the Wings of Love, was published in April 2016. His future projects include writing a novel.

A FAKE STONE

I also could have been a gem

Shiny, dazzling and glimmering,

If she had sawn my rough edges

Like a connoisseur does

That makes a stone glittering.

But she mistook me for a fake stone

And, I was derisively thrown

On the very path

Where she daily walks

Up and down

To her town

Very candidly;

And I chose to creep silently

To my dark cave

A Fake Stone

Amidst the path's bricks

Not for the fear of her kicks

But for caring her feet

As her walk is very naive

While on the street,

And her feet softer than the grass

Would not get hurt erroneously

Lest it would add only another pain

To my ever bleeding heart..!

"But she mistook me for a fake stone,

and, I was derisively thrown..."

YOU SCALED THE SKIES

No wonder you scaled the skies,

No wonder you upset oceans,

No wonder you moved mountains

But wouldn't it be a great wonder

If you scaled the heart,

The heart that cares not for you,

If you could plant the emotion

Of love in that heart?

YOUR SILENCE

Your silence slowly kills me

In this dark stormy night

I try to take on the battle

But I feel losing the fight

Beauty is hidden though in silence

If it were the silence of soul

But greater beauty I do find

In thy soothing words as whole

For, thy words of wild wisdom

Pour nectar in my ears

And my heart feels liberated

From the shackles of unknown fears.

If you want me to be in silence

Let me fall asleep

On thy cosy bosom

Under the shelter of thy silky hair

Where on I can lay for ages

A Fake Stone

In the utmost tranquillity

Ignoring the laws and ethics

And the rules of morality.

PASSION

I love thy passion

And the deep set expression,

That the day and night you say

In an unprecedented fashion,

"Of the love and longing un-beat

Let's wait for the Day

When our two souls and bodies

Shall mingle with melting heat

Leaving behind all dismay!"

SHE WAS TIRED OF WAITING

The dawn is silently creeping,

But my darling is still sleeping,

For she was tired of waiting

For her sweetheart.

Last night he stayed far apart

And reaching from there was too hard.

Yet she waited all night,

Might he come to her in a dream,

And passionately hug her tight.

She smiles, her sleep full of innocent fun

As the beams of the rising sun

Embrace the horizon in a gleam.

FRUSTRATION

This world is very frustrating.

One moment is brimmed with glee,

And the next is flooded with pain.

The ways of world are very tormenting

I always fail to sustain.

Weary days, scary nights,

Deadly dark and fearing sights,

Vague images, masked faces

Make me shake in sheer fright,

And lead me to disdain.

Either it is my inborn nature

Or my perceptions are wrong,

I fail to fathom literature

That defines the right or wrong,

But one thing is more than surer

Me is a very lone creature,

In myriad crowds all along

I beg to thee my Creator.

THE SPRING

Winter gone, came sober sunshine.

Fragrance came, came sublime

On the face of nature Queen

As the spring had there been.

Birds began to sing and chime

And the day seemed so fine

That it had so never been

For sweet melodies this spring

My heart wished to sing

With matching notes to the birds.

As I felt fantasies for ever

Of my darling's swing hair

As if fragrance blended in air

Of nectar body odour

Of my darling dear!

"Winter gone,
Came sober sunshine."

HOW BRUTAL COULD YOU BE?

How brutal could you ever be!

What wrong had I committed

If I longed for thee?

Divine rules can't be limited

Within the range of social decree.

Craving for opposite being

Is universal law in nature.

If you don't believe my viewing

You can consult literature

Untrue it can never be.

See the river and the sea,

See the flower and the bee,

See the clouds and the rain,

See the moth and the flame

They all seem tempted to mingle

Then why should I be single?

I TRIED TO BE A FLOWER

I tried to be a flower

Hoping she would decor me

In her silky hair,

But with a trick unfair

She chose to undo her hair

And I got withered.

I tried to be collyrium,

And got to dwell in her eyes

But she shed me out

With tears of her joyful cries,

Mocking at my saddening sighs.

Then I chose to be crimson

And hoped she would wear me

On her forehead

But she wiped me out

With contempt

And wore a red thread.

A Fake Stone

At last I mixed in dust,

To be gently ravaged

Under her soft feet

For where I can get her touches

Without being endangered

Of separation.

VALENTINE

As the spring set in the air

And the weather seemed so fine

He said with a joy sublime,

"It's you that keeps me up all night

The one getting me through the day

And so it seems to me that there

Is only one thing left to say.

I don't know how to deal it

To make it sound so true

So I'll say it how I feel it

I'm completely in love with you,

Will you be my valentine..?"

She said with a chime,

"Well, it sounds so fine,

You are the dimple in my cheek,

The tingle in my soul.

A Fake Stone

The voice that makes me weak,

You're the one that makes me whole.

I will be your valentine."

Let my soul be mingle with thine

For you my heart sings sweetly

Do come and lie by me

The sand does part so neatly

As we lie beside the sea."

And thus they both sang and rejoiced

All the delicacies of love

But the fate had other design.

On the next valentine

They repeated the same words

But to different persons.

LORD KRISHNA

Never born it is and never dies

No becoming has, it does not cease

Unborn, ageless, constant, timeless,

Killed it can't be though its body is."

That the weapon cannot cut

Nor the raging fire singe,

Neither can the water wet

Nor dry it becomes in the wind."

Beyond cleaving, beyond burning

Beyond drying, beyond drenching

All pervading, immovable

That stands eternal and stable."

If you however think this one

On births and deaths is ever borne

Even then O valorous one..!

No cause there is for you to mourn.

MY SMITTEN HEART

As I see your scarlet lips,

Scarlet as the sun that slips

Under the horizon,

My nerves feel as if shaking

With an imaginary kiss

Containing my passion.

Though I am amidst a crowd

Of unknown faces,

I feel as if I am in your arms,

Enraptured by your charms,

Drinking in all your graces,

The ecstasy that fills

My smitten heart

LOVE IMMORTAL

Mortality is the law of nature

As birth doeth meet to death,

Nothing can evade this certainty

Either be it your tranquillity

Or the anguish, anger or wrath.

Nativity is sure to embrace infinity.

So the things around are mortal

Yet two things I perceive eternal:

One is your imagined beauty

And the other is my immortal love

In this very mortal world.

And that is so for a valid reason

Your beauty is yet unborn

As it never met to my eye

And it dwells only in my vision.

And my love being immaterialized

Is just an unborn emotion

Both of them are only in notion

And notion is never to die.

THE ROSE

The rose that I picked for you

Now has withered as waiting

For you; for years that seemed ages

Petals are tired of crying

For your soft soothing touches

That might gently caress them.

Alas! You didn't turn around,

Be cruel as you are.

Yet another rose will wait

For you another day,

And many more days to come

Till you pick it up

And adorn your hair.

"Yet another rose will wait

For you another day"

LOVE IS NOT MERELY TO...

"Love is not merely to cry for someone in the depth of the heart,

But also to feel the presence of the beloved within the body, mind and spirit even

With the sad perception that the person you love will never be yours."

ILL-FATED BIRDS (MAKE A LOUD NOISE)

Make a loud noise, O ill-fated birds!

Your noise, your only weapon

May drive away the fowler,

Recognise the killer.

The poster-boy himself is a hawk

Who may hinder your flight

Before you take off.

My hands are shorter,

Yet larger are my resolutions!

No dream, neither a promise

To build a safe shelter for you,

Neither a hope to build a Taj

Of yours or my dreams,

Yet to live is necessary,

For life is necessary

And necessary is to save

The necessary things

A Fake Stone

Of necessary life.

Let the rulers get to hell,

And their brokers too.

In your share is only noise,

And in mine only the pen

To save you from the darker den,

In the democracy

So make a loud noise

It's the only weapon you have

To save yourselves!

IN THE MIDDLE OF THE NIGHT

In the middle of the night,

Dark becomes beautifully bright

When I feel thy divine presence,

Lost I get into ecstasy,

Away from any notion or sense.

In the middle of the night,

I drown in fantasy,

Riding on the flight of love

That transports me into lunacy,

Yet so soothing is thy presence

In the middle of the night!

"In your arms lies my heaven… "

IN YOUR ARMS

In your laughs lies my pleasure,

And in your eyes, my shadows.

In your arms lies my heaven,

And in your pain, my sorrows.

In your humility lies my peace,

And in your disdain, my despair.

Hidden are many treasures

Within your embrace,

Yet solace does also hid there,

In the shadow of thy silky hair.

WHEN LOVE BECOMES HATE

The soul gets shattered into pieces,

The heart discards all the preaches,

The mind does work but underrate,

When love converts in hate.

The world seems be an enemy,

The life feels as hellish and gloomy,

Actions look as if inanimate,

And thoughts lose their weight,

When love converts in hate.

Yet the sixth sense wants to wait

For the beloved soul mate!

HOW PATHETIC

How pathetic scheme of nature!

The desert is missing the rain,

And the rain is missing the clouds!

The clouds are missing the showers

And the showers are sobbing in pain.

My heart is missing my maiden

And my hopes are missing the shrouds.

THE SCARS

In the depth of dead emotions,

There is still too much pain.

Wounds though healed are weary,

Scars are yet to sustain,

And I feel all around me

A free flow, like a rain of pain,

As the scars create a void in

Newer wounds through the pores,

Sending me in dismal disdain.

Yet my heart has learnt to rejoice,

In this rain of severe pain,

As it has made a discovery

Beauty does persist in pain.

MY SHARE

I sincerely did try

To sustain and uphold

The earth and the sky

Of mine share

But the earthly bondages

Snatched away the earth

Of my share

And left for me the sky

Leaving me half in cages

And when i got finally liberated

From the shackles of the relations

I found to my dismay

The sky too was not mine.

WALKING ALONE IN THE DARK

Walking alone in the dark and dew,

I came across a shadow unknown.

My crumbling heart prompted me,

To touch it with an impulse drawn,

I couldn't believe my eyes as it neared,

It was my own fear of the unknown.

"It was my own fear of the unknown."

LET THEM THINK WHAT THEY WILL

Let them think what they think

Let them freak, bleak or blink

I am not going to change

Let them reek, seek or sink

Let them hail, fail or pink

Change is now beyond my range

I have set my nerves to link

With the phrases and the ink

That redefines the word "revenge"

That sent me to the brink

Of becoming an infamous kink

WHEN

When loves dies, there are no winners

Only two losers who did not care enough.

And like a river with turbulent waters,

The parting of two hearts is always rough.

THE DYING SOUL

My worn out soul is knocking loudly,

Knocking at Thy heaven's door

O let my soul also be there!

Dancing, singing and merrymaking

On Thy divine celestial floor;

For ages, I've been suffering

In the dark of dismal den,

Lurking shadows of death so fearing

Poor soul crying with pain!!

In this weary and cruel world,

Pleasures were, but were so rare

And even these were lost in despair,

In the dark of brutal world!

And plenty of piercing pains;

A Fake Stone

For, I always favoured the fair

Barring all the gains unfair,

For, I never wished to dare

To disobey Thy rules so fine,

Inscribed as they are there

In Thy holy books divine;

As I've heard the sages' say

"Those who follow Thy holy rules

Shall always in heaven dwell,

And those who disobey thy order

Shall perish in depth of hell..!"

Me, as a holy child

Sacred as thy sacred words,

Lying on my death bed today,

Beg for Thy mercy mild,

O! Let my bleeding soul sneak

In the dawn of thy divine door..!

A Fake Stone

The shackled soul in body so weak

Is straining to get liberated

From the fetters of worldly affairs;

O! Let my soul be buried in peace,

No, let's no more be delayed,

For, I always found myself there,

Looted, cheated and betrayed

In the realms of the mortal world.

"O! let my soul be buried in peace

Looted, cheated and betrayed

In the realms of mortal world"

NO END TO FLIGHTS

No end to heights,

Even after the end there is much to fly,

As much as shorter falls the sky.

And no end to the sky

Even after the end there is much sky

In which shorter fall flights..!

But see the outcome of courage

Miracle is bound to happen

When you will dare to try.

No end to courage

Even after the end there is much to try..!

There happen flights, let them be.

There are the skies, let them be.

And there are temptations to dare,

Let them be

Someday all will be so right,

No good to fall victim of care,

A Fake Stone

Hold the head straight upright,

The course of life can be altered

Just dare to try beyond your might.

THE LAMP OF WISDOM (HAPPY DEEPAWALI)

Let's celebrate the Festival of Light

With a sacred pure heart,

Light a lamp of wisdom so bright,

The dark of ignorance be torn apart,

A lamp of kindness and sympathy,

A lamp of brotherhood and apathy,

A lamp of hard work and prosperity,

A lamp of tolerance and gentility,

Even for the downtrodden..!

O light as many as you can,

The lamps of love and care,

Of serenity and devotion

To brighten your heaven abode,

And a lamp of forbearance

And co-operation

Be fixed over above

A Fake Stone

Your sweet emotion..!

Let there be no darkness,

Inside, outside, fore and hind

Above, under or beneath

Your sweet home,

And above the horizon,

Of your mind

Light a lamp of sacred thought

To unleash the spark of tranquillity,

For peace of mind is all that counts

Over, above all prosperity..!!

Happy Deepawali.

"O light as many as you can,

The lamps of love and care,

Of serenity and devotion

To brighten your heaven abode…"

© Charu Porush

THE COURSE OF LIFE

What is the course of life?

Of mortal men on earth,

We are born and so we die

Many of us struggling dearth,

With valour that not to defy.

Yet most men eddy about,

Here and there-eat and drink,

Chatter and love and hate are raised

Aloof and hurled in the dust,

Striving, blindly achieving

Nothing and missing the brink.

Perish and no one asks

Who or what they have been...

And there are some rarely found

Whom a thirst ardent; unquenchable fixes

Not with a crowd to be spent

A Fake Stone

Not without aim to go round

In an eddy of purposely dust

Effort unmeaning and vain

Ah yes- some of us strive

Not without an action to die

Fruitless, but something to snatch

For the sake of a mere snatch

From dull oblivion of endless path

Leading all but to the grave...!!

THE CLOCK OF LIFE

The clock of life is wound but once,

And no one has the power

To tell just when the hands will stop,

At late or early hour;

Now is the only time you own

To Live, love and toil with a will.

Place no faith in tomorrow, for

The clock of life then may be still..!

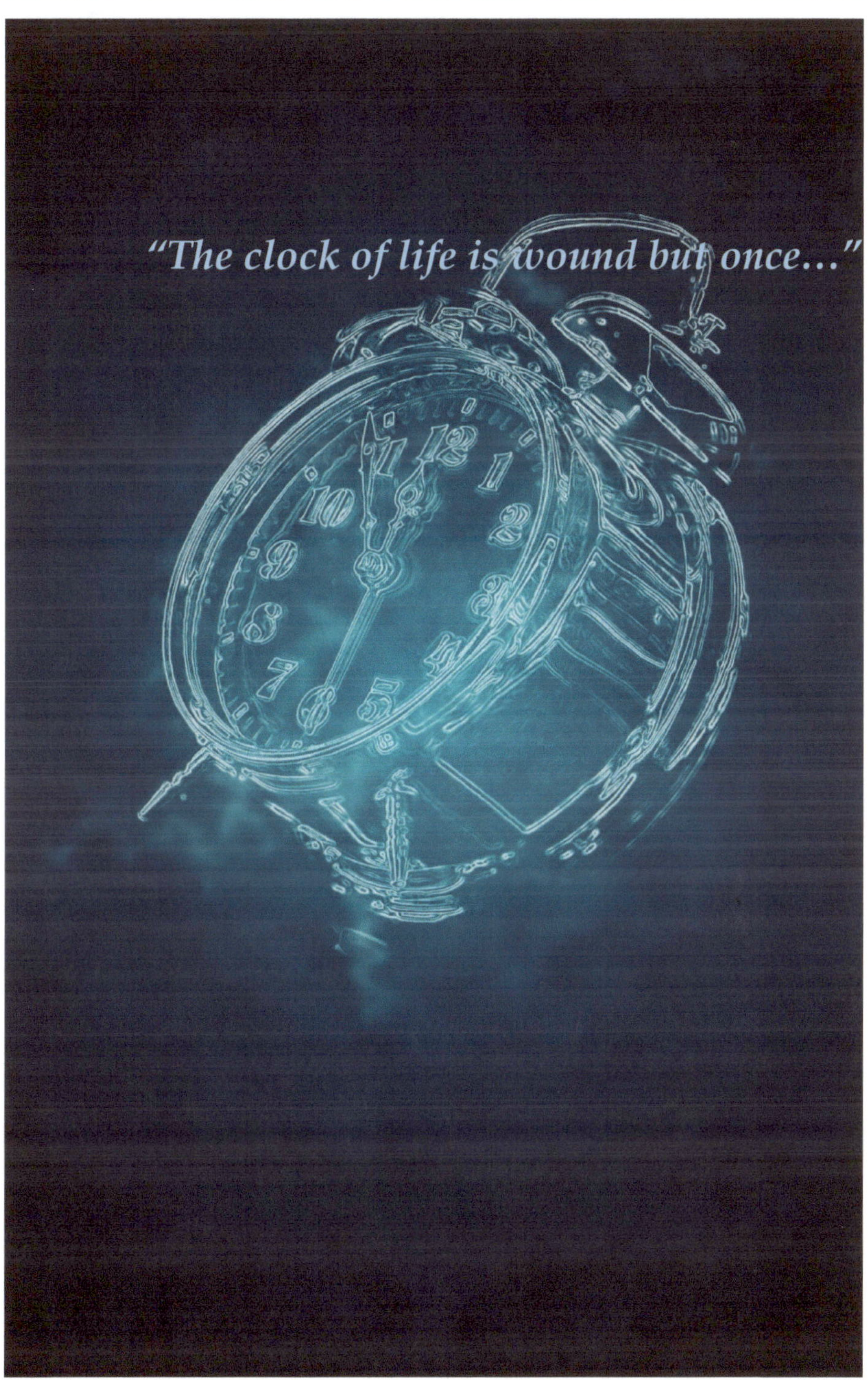
"The clock of life is wound but once..."

I DO NOT NEED

I do not need palaces

To dwell in peace and pleasure.

Just your arms with caresses

Would suffice more than any treasure,

Where I seek solaces

From the worldly pressure

Of striving hard for nothing.

I do not need to conquer

The vast lands of fertility

To attain the prosperity.

Just a loving corner in your heart

Would suffice to make me feel

Pleasure beyond eternity.

I do not need to please

The gods and the goddesses,

Enchanting sacred hymns

A Fake Stone

To ensure my salvation.

I just want to whisper

Sweet songs of love and passion,

And it will be more than enough

To reserve a place in heaven.

I NEVER WISHED TO HURT HER

I never wished to hurt her heart,

Neither did I, ever.

But fate played its part,

As destiny being so clever

Turned her longing into hate,

Leaving me battered.

Even worse that she seems shattered

And granting me no rebate.

Now my sole motto in life

Seems as if to turn destiny,

As they say it's never late

To struggle and strife.

IF

If my ink was water

The seven seas wouldn't be sufficient

To contain the caring words I've written.

Oh such deep feelings can't falter,

For Love is forever omniscient

Of the secrets my heart has hidden.

Should I tell her that alone at night,

I often turn my face to the moon

Whispering a prayer for her happiness?

Should I tell her of my soul's delight?

For her love is an auspicious monsoon

That pulled me out of my distress?

If the stars were my words

The sky would not be vast enough

To contain all the love I feel.

I dream of her arms curled

Around me. Though of shyness I would blush,

She would sense all the desires I conceal.

A Fake Stone

If my ink was a bed

It couldn't contain the passion I can't crush.

Head bowed, before her I would kneel,

Humbled, never wanting our story to end.

SINGLE

Single I was born on the planet

Single as I yet have to dwell.

Being single is my destiny

Single I will perish in hell

Yet a single wish is there

In the depth of withered heart

And a flash of hope in eyes

That someday when I am to die

My lady in the dark will come

To mourn and wail in cries.

"Single I was born on the planet..."

AND SO WE DIE

We are born and so we die,

Alas! What's the stuff we are made of?

We never leave to tell a lie..!!

HIS FACEBOOK GIRL

Her gaze caught him unaware,

For an instant, nothing existed

But her soft stare.

He was lost, totally subjugated.

Her insolent beauty, like a queen

Had him enthralled and tortured.

She flaunted her sweet eighteen,

He was a lamb slaughtered.

Unable to look away.

He became her lover that year.

Though he knew he was led astray,

To lose her was his biggest fear.

Did she love him or did she play

Him? She knew he couldn't be free,

She toyed with him, hopeless prey,

Of his destruction, she was the key.

I wonder if he still cries for her,

A Fake Stone

Alone, at night, if he is wishing

For his Facebook girl to reappear?

Does he still search for her, hoping…?

Written in cooperation with FSamuel,

inspired by Lokendra's forthcoming novel.

"For an instant, nothing existed,
But her soft stare."

REFLECTIONS...

"Where there is Love there stands the beauty of the Taj, where there is Hatred, there remains the Holocaust.

 Let us unite together in an unbreakable bond to create beautiful things for ourselves and those around us."

© Lokendra Porush

Thank you for reading A Fake Stone by Lokendra Porush. We hope you have enjoyed it and we would appreciate it if you could leave constructive feedback on Amazon.co.uk, Goodreads.com or Lulu.com

You can also contact us at:

fnvPublications@gmail.com

Francine P. Samuel

A Fake Stone

FNV Publications
3rd Floor
86-90 Paul Street
London EC2A 4NE
United Kingdom